The Art of Laziness

Library Mindset

Also by Library Mindset

100 Quotes That Will Change Your Life

100 Harsh Truths of Life

© 2023 Library Mindset. All rights reserved.

No part of this publication may be reproduced, distributed, or transmitted in any form or by any means, including photocopying, recording, or other electronic or mechanical methods, without the prior written permission of the publisher, except as permitted by copyright law - other than for "fair use" as brief quotations embodied in articles and reviews without prior written permission of the publisher.

The information in this book should not be treated as a substitute for professional medical advice; always consult a medical practitioner. Any use of information in this book is at the reader's discretion and risk. Neither the author nor the publisher can be held responsible for any loss, claim, or damage arising from the use or misuse of the suggestions made, the failure to take medical advice, or any material on third-party websites.

"One day you will wake up, and there won't be any more time to do the things you've always wanted. Do it now."

- Paulo Coelho

Contents

Introduction   1

Part 1: Mindset

100% Responsibility   7
Comfort Zone Is Your Enemy   17
Work on the Right Things   32
Don't Be a Perfectionist   37
Don't be Mediocre!   40
The Myth of Multitasking   44
Daily Routine   48
Learn To Say No   53
Don't Work 24/7   56
Don't Wait   60
Surround Yourself with the Right People   66
Don't Worry   70
Do the Hard Thing First   73
Delegate   78
How To Learn Anything Faster   80

Part 2: Tips & Techniques

20 Productivity Tips I Wish I Had Known Earlier	84
80/20 Rule	84
The Parkinson's Law	84
8 Japanese Techniques to Overcome Laziness	88
Do This For 10 Minute Before You Sleep	92
10 Tiny Habits That Will Change Your Life	95
Pomodoro Technique	99
5 Minute Rule	1011
Two Day Rule	101
Wake Up!	104
Notes	108

Introduction

Life is short.

Hours are passing. Days are passing. Months are passing. Years are passing. Let's say you will live for 100 years. If you're lucky, the average life expectancy in the world is only 72 years (around 3,700 weeks). It may look like a long time, but it's not. And if you are a 30-year-old, you have already spent 1,500 weeks. I am telling you this not to make you sad or to give you an existential crisis but to make you aware that we don't have as much time as we think we have.

We should make the best use of the time we are given. We already know that and have been told that thousands of times, but do we make the best use of our time? Do you love the things that you do? Are you around with the people you love? Life is short for doing the things you hate or not doing the things you want to do. The regret will be huge when you're old. Imagine you're almost 80, looking back at things and wishing you did something differently. You lived a life how you wanted, not how others wanted. You will regret all the moments you wasted being lazy, sitting on a couch watching T.V. for no reason, spending hours daily scrolling social media with no purpose. No person who doesn't do the things that he wants to can be happy from the inside.

Think for a few minutes: what would you regret when you're 80 years old?

Here are a few regrets that you might have:

1. Not doing what you love.

2. Being lazy and wasting your time.

3. Not spending more time with your family.

4. Not taking care of your health and wellbeing.

5. Working hard for nothing in return.

6. Not traveling when you're young.

7. Not enjoying your life to the fullest.

Stop making excuses why you can't do the things you want to. Stop these things right now. Stop giving answers to your mind; start asking questions. It will force your mind to find a way.

Wasting your time so that time can be perfect is the worst excuse, and you will regret it later. There is no perfect time. The best time is now.

If you want to travel the world, now is the best time.

If you want to start a business, now is the best time.

If you want to go to the gym, now is the best time.

You will thank yourself later.

The goal should be to live the best we can. And there are so many things that we are doing every day that we will regret in the future.

This book will be short. My goal is to make you more aware of your daily actions and how they will impact you in the future. After reading this book, I hope you will stop being so lazy and finally start doing what you want.

The book is divided into two parts; the first focuses on your mindset and how you can live a better and more peaceful life, and the second focuses on tips and techniques that will help you overcome laziness and boost your productivity.

Time is running out. Start living now.

Part 1
Mindset

"If you spend your time chasing butterflies, they'll fly away. But if you spend time making a beautiful garden, the butterflies will come.

Don't chase, attract."

100% Responsibility

"The price of greatness is responsibility."
−Winston Churchill

It's useless to blame something else for all your problems. You can blame your friends, family, spouse, or anyone else. The good thing that blaming others does is that it makes us feel good from the inside by convincing our minds that we can't do anything in this situation, but that's wrong. There's always something that you can do. Even if you can't change the situation, you can always do the best possible thing.

Blaming others does nothing. It doesn't solve your problem. Let's say you blame your friends, family, job, or anything else for not having enough time to exercise. You can condemn the whole world. All the blame in the world will not help you find time to exercise. If you want to find a solution, you will find it; it's not that a solution doesn't exist. It exists, and you know it deep inside of your heart. Only action can help you achieve your goals, nothing else. No one can help you achieve your goals.

Nobody cares if you're lazy or not.

Nobody cares if you procrastinate or not.

Nobody cares if you exercise or not.

Why would they care? Nobody cares. It would be best for you if you do things for yourself. You must act. You must find time.

It is easier to sit on the couch and watch TV than go for a run.

It's easier to scroll on social media than to read a book.

It' easier to procrastinate than to work hard.

Our mind always goes towards the easy option. You need to change it to choose the best choice for yourself, not the easy one.

Library Mindset

We blame all the time to avoid confronting our problems because it's super easy to blame. You blame someone else, and boom, you no longer think that maybe you can do something about it. Every action that you take or not take impacts your life. So, the next time you blame someone else for your problem, consider the consequences. Your future is in the hands of your present actions.

Don't even think about the past. It's already gone. There are only two things that the past can give you: lessons and regrets.

Learn from the past, but don't let him have too much control over your life. Learn from your mistakes. There's nothing wrong with making a mistake, but if you keep repeating the same error, there is something wrong. Don't be stupid. Neither love nor hate mistakes. If you hate mistakes, then you become fearful of them. You start to overthink. It destroys your peace of mind. It doesn't allow you to take action. If you love mistakes, you start making more because you attract what you love.

If a mistake happens, learn from it and move on. Don't waste your time. If you're not moving forward, you're making a second mistake.

Harsh truths of life:

If you're lazy, it's your fault.

If you're unhappy, it's your fault.

If you're a procrastinator, it's your fault.

What are you going to gain by escaping from the responsibility? Nothing. If you want to change something about your life, you must fully know you're responsible for your actions. The things that you want to achieve can only be achieved by yourself. Nobody else can do it for you. Complaining achieves nothing. It fills your mind with worry and negative thoughts. Overthinking and complaining all the time is terrible for your mental health. You need to act. You can start today, or you can wait till tomorrow. The choice is yours.

"The best time to plant a tree was 20 years ago. The second-best time is now." -Chinese proverb

Mistakes aren't as bad as you think

It's okay that you made a mistake. When you're doing something, mistakes are bound to happen. It's normal. But you must take responsibility for your mistakes. You are responsible for all the actions that you do. Learn from your mistakes and move on. Speed is necessary if you want to move forward with your life. You can't sit there and keep thinking about your mistakes.

If you're not a lazy person who sits all day and does nothing, then mistakes will happen. You can't sit there, afraid of making mistakes; you must jump into the unknown.

"Success does not consist in never making mistakes but in never making the same one a second time."

- George Bernard Shaw

Stick to your business

This simple tip will make you more productive: Don't worry if it's not your business. If something doesn't affect you, don't worry about it. People are constantly worrying about things that don't impact them. Keep yourself focused on what is truly your concern. You're the most important person in your life, so make it your goal to do your best for yourself. Stop worrying about other people's opinions. 99% of the opinions you hear are wrong and will not help you. Trust in yourself.

"Keep your attention focused entirely on what is truly your concern and be clear that what belongs to others is their business and none of yours."-
Epictetus

Nobody is coming to save you

No one can change your life. Nobody has any interest in changing your life. Their own life is a mess, so how can they change yours? You must do it yourself. It's in your own hands. You can be lazy and wait for others to help, but you will wait forever. Get this out of your head that somebody else can help you achieve your goals. Stop being dependent on other people. You have the power to choose whether you want to remain lazy or want to do something meaningful in life.

Here's a great fictional story of a farmer:

Once there was a farmer. He had a wheat farm. But there was a sparrow nest in his wheat farm, and there were four little children of that sparrow in that nest. The Sparrow used to go daily in the forest to feed her little children.

Library Mindset

One day, when she returned from the forest, she found their children were terrified. She asked them what had happened and why they were so scared. They said the farmer had come here today and discussed wheat harvesting. He said he would send his sons to cut the crops tomorrow. They said where they will go after crops have been cut. After listening to their children, the sparrow said that nobody would come tomorrow to cut the wheat crops, so don't be scared.

The next day, the same happened, as Sparrow said. No one came there to cut the crops. Many days passed, but no one came there to cut the crops. Everything was going well. Sparrow's children were very happy.

One day, when Sparrow returned from the forest, she was again shocked by seeing her children's faces. They were so scared again. Sparrow asked them the reason behind their fear. They again said the farmer had come here today and discussed crop harvesting. Today, he said he would send the laborers to cut the crops tomorrow. After listening to them, Sparrow again told them not to worry; no one would come tomorrow.

The next day, again, the same happened as Sparrow said. No one came there to cut the crops. Furthermore, many days passed. But no one came there to cut the crops.

The Art of Laziness

Again, one day, the sparrow returned from the forest, and she saw her children's scared faces again. She asked again about their fear. They said the farmer came here again today and talked about wheat harvesting. But today, he said he has wasted a lot of time depending on others, and he said that tomorrow, he will come to cut the crops by himself. After listening to this, the sparrow said, tomorrow, we will leave this place and make our nest in some other place. Sparrow told their children that tomorrow he would cut the wheat crops. That's why we must leave this place.

The next day, the same happened as the sparrow said. The farmer came there and cut the crops. After seeing this, the sparrow's little children asked his mother if whatever you said went right every time. What was the reason behind this?

Sparrow said the farmer was dependent upon his sons the first time and the second time he was dependent upon laborers. That's why the work was not completed.

But the third time, he was not dependent upon anyone. That's why he succeeded this time.

Library Mindset

3 Types of People:

There are three types of people I see all around me:

1. The first one is the majority of people; they never start. They never do anything. They sit there and be lazy. They never work on their dreams. They never do what they are supposed to do. They are just waiting for something good to happen.

2. The second type of people are those who start, but as soon as things get hard, they give up, and then they regret why they gave up.

3. The third type of people are those who work hard, don't give up despite hardships, and keep going. They are the one percent who do become successful.

One must be persistent. Things aren't always smooth. Things can go wrong and will go wrong. Your path will have obstacles, but you must progress toward your goals.

Life is not a sprint but a marathon. It's long and hard. There is no reward for the quitters who quit halfway. You must reach the finish line to achieve something.

Control What You Can Control

You must be aware of what you can and can't control. Don't become sad when things which you can't control don't work according to your plan. Don't confuse what you can and can't control. Not everything is out of your control. There are a lot of things that you can control that will improve your life. You have control over your mind. You have control over the amount of hard work you do. But you have no control over what other people will think about you. Worrying about things you can't control will make your life miserable.

Comfort Zone Is Your Enemy

"A comfort zone is a beautiful place, but nothing ever grows there." - Unknown

One of the biggest reasons people are lazy and always want to do everything tomorrow is because they are too comfortable with their lives. They don't want to change the way things are going. Doing the things that you're always doing is easy, but it doesn't lead to the growth that you want.

Growth demands that you step out of your comfort zone and do the hard things. It's easy to watch movies, read news, and scroll social media all day, but it's not meaningful, and you know it. Your body knows that you're wasting your time. That's why you feel bad after you waste your time that could be used for something valuable and meaningful.

Do you want to spend your entire life wasting your time? Time is running out. Soon, you will genuinely not have the energy to do what you want. Do them now. Stop waiting for something to happen automatically. Nothing is going to happen; you must make it happen.

After leaving their comfort zone, nobody says that they wish they stayed there. You will feel blissful after you stop procrastinating and start doing what you want. Nothing gives you more happiness than waking up every day with the energy to start working on the things you want to do.

Keep it Simple!

Whenever you're trying to do something new, always try to keep it as simple as possible. Don't try to do too much at one time. Don't overthink about all the things that can go wrong. Most of the time, they don't go wrong at all. What you should do is to start as soon as possible. You need to have urgency. The urge to do things fast. Not urgency in getting the desired results but the urgency in doing the work. Let's say you want to learn how to create a website. You can start right now, or you can keep waiting.

Your first plan never works; you need to make adjustments. You may even need to change your plan altogether. Do it and do it as fast as possible. Speed is crucial. You don't have as much time as you think you have. Keep things simple and do things with lightning speed.

"Most decisions should probably be made with somewhere around 70 percent of the information you wish you had...if you wait for 90 percent, in most cases, you're probably being slow."
-Jeff Bezos

Start to think a little bit differently!

"If everyone is thinking alike, then somebody isn't thinking." - George S. Patton

You do not need to think just like everyone else. You can judge for yourself. You can think like no one else, and it is entirely okay.

You must think and do different things than anyone else to get different results. You can't do what everybody else is doing and expect different results. You can't do what you have been doing in the past and predict a different outcome this time. Most of the time, the outcome is the same. If you're lazy, you know the result, just like the last time.

Set Clear Goals

We should set clear goals that are both possible and can be achieved quickly. Setting huge, ambitious goals is not bad, but the problem is if you're a super lazy person, you will not work toward that goal because it would seem too hard and impossible to achieve.

That's why in the start you should set small easy goals that can be achieved.
Goals should also be clear. For example, a clear goal is that you want to lose 2 kilograms in 1 month. An unclear goal is that you want to be healthy.
A goal that can't be measured and has no time duration is not a goal. You're just expecting a miracle to happen.

Write down your goals

If you don't write down your goals on paper, you should start doing it now; you will not regret it. If you have clearly written goals and read them regularly, they will motivate you. You will feel some guilt if you don't do what you have written. Even if you achieve half of your goals, that's still better than doing nothing.

Don't Overcomplicate

I'm not a big fan of all the various apps that people use to measure their productivity. I think it's a complete waste of time. You don't need any app to focus on your goals. I prefer writing things. You only need two things: pen and paper. That's it. Don't overcomplicate simple stuff.

Anything more than that is just a waste of energy.

You Will Regret It Later

When we don't do what we actually want to do and instead procrastinate, that thing keeps bothering us. It doesn't allow us to live in peace because we subconsciously know that we are lazy and should do that task, but we don't.

Think Long Term

You can do two things. You can think long-term and do things that will be valuable for you in the long term, or you can satisfy your short-term pleasures and ignore the future.

One should have in mind how the actions that they take in the present are going to affect the future. One thing that I can tell you for sure is that you will always regret being lazy. Laziness feels good in the present as it gives an immediate dopamine hit. Doing something new is hard and doesn't give an instant dopamine hit, but in the future, you will always regret being lazy and never doing things that you want to do.

You need to delay instant gratification, do hard things, take some stress, and make sacrifices so that you can achieve your future goals.

I'm not telling you not to avoid all fun in the present entirely, but sometimes short sacrifices are necessary for a better future.

Take Risk

Don't be afraid of risks. If you want to achieve anything in your life, you must jump from a comfortable position to an uncomfortable position. The regret of not taking a risk is enormous. You are going to regret your entire life if you don't take risks. Taking risks is scary and should be, but not taking risks is even scarier,

"The biggest risk is not taking any risk... In a world that is changing really quickly, the only strategy that is guaranteed to fail is not taking risks."
- Mark Zuckerberg

No Good, No Bad

Stop thinking everything is either good or bad. There are a lot of bad things that happened to me, and I'm happy now that they happened to me as they changed the trajectory of my life. Here's a great story:

There was a farmer with a horse who helped him in farming. The villagers constantly told the farmer how lucky he was to have such a great horse.

"Maybe," he would reply.

One day, the horse ran away. The villagers came to the farmer to express their sympathies.

"That's too bad." the villagers said.

"Maybe," the farmer replied.

A few days later, the horse returned home with ten strong wild horses.

"That's great, isn't it?" the villagers said.

"Maybe," the farmer again replied.

The next day, the farmer's son was riding one of the horses when it kicked him off and broke his leg.

The villagers arrived to express their dismay.

"That's too bad," they said.

"Maybe," the farmer replied.

A military officer marched into the village the next day, recruiting able-bodied young men for the war.

The Art of Laziness

The farmer's son, with his broken leg, was left behind.

The villagers were joyful, "Your son has been spared. What beautiful luck!"

The farmer smiled.

"Maybe."

Self-Discipline

"We must all suffer from one of two pains: the pain of discipline or the pain of regret." – Jim Rohn

Self-discipline means doing the things that are good for your future but are hard to do in the present.

Going to the gym is hard, but sitting on the couch is easy.

It's hard to start a business, but it's easy to procrastinate.

It's hard to read books but easy to watch movies.

It's hard to wake up early but easy to lay in a warm bed.

All things that are going to improve your life are hard. Always ask yourself this question:

Will I regret not doing this in the future?

If the answer is yes, it must be done no matter how hard it is.

Do what needs to be done

"There's no shortage of remarkable ideas; what's missing is the will to execute them." – Seth Godin

Discipline means doing anything that needs to be done. If this means working hard, then you will work harder. If it means working smarter, then you will be working smarter. Never avoid doing the things you want to do just because they're hard.

Procrastination is the enemy of discipline

Procrastination means avoiding doing a task that needs to be done by giving excuses to do it later. Without giving excuses, you will feel bad, and we don't want to feel bad, so we give different types of excuses. The most popular one is "I'm waiting for the right time." The time will never be right; it can't be perfect. There are always going to be obstacles in your way. Many things will try their best to make you lazy and procrastinate, but you must overcome all of them.

Delay Gratification

It's hard to delay gratification because we want to enjoy things now. Nothing is wrong with it, but the problem arises when you do things that harm your future. Actions that you will regret in the future, and you will be asking yourself why did I do that?

You must look in both directions: present and future. You must enjoy the present but not at the cost of your future. By being lazy, you don't enjoy both your present and future.

Do It Now!

"Only put off until tomorrow what you are willing to die having left undone" - Pablo Picasso

The time is never going to be perfect. If it becomes perfect, then there is a chance that it's already too late. You can wait all you want; nothing will happen, or you can start today and move towards achieving your goals. You can't wait for the perfect time, better resources, or more experience. Even if you don't have a perfect plan with all the details, you can start today and figure things out along the way.

There are no hacks

Stop looking for an easy way out. You can know all the tiny tips and hacks, but you must do the work. A lot of people are just way too focused on learning than doing. Learning is great but alone it will not be enough. You must put in the work to get things done. Stop looking for hacks before you even begin. First, start and then learn about various methods to do things faster.

Don't Let Failure Stop You

There are always ups and downs in life. Sometimes, you're doing great; sometimes, you're not. Here is a great story:

Once, a king called upon all of his wise men and asked them, is there a mantra or suggestion that works in every situation, circumstance, place, and time? In every joy, every sorrow, every defeat, and every victory? One answer for all questions

All the wise men were puzzled by the King's question. An old man suggested something that appealed to all of them. They went to the king and gave him something written on paper, with the condition that the king would not see it out of curiosity.

Only in extreme danger, when the King finds himself alone, and there seems to be no way, can he see it. The King put the papers under his Diamond ring.

Sometime later, the neighbors attacked the Kingdom. King and his army fought bravely but lost the battle. The King had to flee on his horse. The enemies were following him and getting closer and closer. Suddenly, the King found himself standing at the end of the road - that road was not going anywhere. Underneath, there was a rocky valley a thousand feet deep. If he jumped into it, he would be finished, and he could not return because it was a small road, and the sound of enemy horses was approaching fast. The King became restless. There seemed to be no way.

Then suddenly he saw the Diamond in his ring shining in the sun and remembered the message hidden in the ring. He opened the diamond and read the message. The message was: THIS TOO SHALL PASS.

The Art of Laziness

The King read it. Again, read it. Suddenly, something struck him- Yes! This too will pass. Only a few days ago, I was enjoying my kingdom. I was the mightiest of all the Kings. Yet today, the Kingdom and all my pleasures have gone. I am here trying to escape from enemies. As those days of luxuries have gone, this day of danger too will pass. A calm came on his face. He kept standing there. The place where he was standing was full of natural beauty. He had never known that such a beautiful place was also a part of his Kingdom.

The revelation of the message had a significant effect on him. He relaxed and forgot about those following him. After a few minutes, he realized that the noise of the horses and the enemy coming was receding. They moved into another part of the mountains and were nowhere near him.

He reorganized his army and fought again. He defeated the enemy and regained his empire. When he returned to his empire after victory, he was received with much fanfare. The whole capital was rejoicing in the victory.

Everyone was in a festive mood. Flowers were being showered on King from every house, from every corner. People were dancing and singing. For a moment, the King said, " I am one of the bravest and greatest Kings. It is not easy to defeat me. Suddenly, the Diamond of his ring flashed in the sunlight, reminding him of the message. He opens it and rereads it: THIS TOO SHALL PASS.

Work on the Right Things

"Even Michelangelo would have trouble getting out of bed if he had nothing but a day of spreadsheets ahead. It's hard to imagine Leonardo da Vinci working for a corporation or being a government bureaucrat." - Vizi Andrew

You should ask yourself whether you're working on the right thing.

There is no point in doing things that shouldn't be done at all. You will always be lazy if you don't love what you do. These are signs by your body that you should try to change your work. Do something meaningful. You can never be motivated to do meaningless things.

If your work is repetitive and has no flavor, finding meaning and happiness in the job would be very hard.

No work is more important than life. You should do what you love but also not run away from the hard part of your work.

Somebody wants to paint, but he becomes an accountant by listening to some people's opinions. The regret of not following his passion will always stay in his mind.

Work Is Happiness

You'll spend a lot of time doing some kind of work. If you don't choose what you want, somebody will choose it for you, and you may not like it. The work selected by others for you will feel like a burden to you but if you choose the work that want to do then you will be blissful. Your work is the pathway to happiness. You can't be happy if you don't like your work. You can never be motivated to work if you don't like your work. If you love your work, there will be no laziness. You will even forget the concept of laziness entirely.

I have one piece of advice for you: if you don't love your work, start finding a way to leave your work as soon as possible. You can never be happy in a sad job. Love what you do. It will make you at ease with existence.

Listen to your inner self; it will guide you.

Don't Run Away from Hard Things

Doing what you love doesn't mean you run away from the complex parts of your job. It doesn't mean you don't give your 100%. It doesn't mean that you become lazy and don't work hard.

Whenever we start doing something new, the motivation is high, and we begin with excitement as soon as the initial motivation wears off. The complex reality of the work starts to appear, problems begin to arise, it becomes more challenging, and then we stop liking our work even though we love it. It's our passion. Following your passion doesn't guarantee that you will always be happy.

When Vincent Van Gogh was 27, he entirely dedicated himself to painting. He used to work with extreme intensity. Painting was his whole life. He was highly productive. He used to paint at lightning speed, but despite his hard work and genius, he struggled financially because his painting wouldn't sell as he was ahead of his time. He was supported mainly financially by his younger brother, Theo Van Gogh. His mental health deteriorated, and on July

27th, 1890, he was painting in a field himself when he shot himself in the chest with a pistol, and two days later, he died.

Learn To Prioritise

You can't do everything. We have limited energy and must spend it in the best way possible. You don't want to spread it too much to risk exhaustion and no results. You're more likely to give up if you see no results and are exhausted too much. You need to focus your energy on selected tasks. The less, the better.

Attract not Chase

Don't chase anything. Don't run after anything. Work to make yourself better so that everything is attracted to you. Focus on yourself. Everything else will take care of itself.

You Are Great!

Stop feeding your mind that you're not good enough to do anything. You can do it. Don't be your own biggest enemy by feeding your mind negative things. Be confident that you can do things. The biggest reason people remain lazy is that they keep thinking that they aren't good enough. You are great. Start doing. In the end, everything will be okay.

Don't Be a Perfectionist

"Perfectionism is a disease. Procrastination is a disease. ACTION is the cure."- Richie Norton

I'm not saying perfection is terrible, but it's not worth it in every part of your life. Beautiful things exist because someone spends much time on tiny details. Without perfection, the world wouldn't be that great. There would be only low-quality things all around us. The world is beautiful both due to its perfection and imperfection.

Leonardo da Vinci was obsessed with tiny details. He would spend years trying to paint a single painting. When designing the Cathedral of Milan, he created hundreds of designs. It took him more than ten years to paint the famous Mona Lisa.

Steve Jobs also had a crazy obsession with details. When designing the first Macintosh computer, he insisted that the circuit board wires should look straight and beautiful even though no one would see the inside as only the technician could open the computer with special tools.

If you're painting or creating something, then yes, it should be as perfect as possible, but if you're doing something like cutting grass, which is going to regrow in a few weeks, don't spend your entire day trying to be a perfectionist and trying to cut each blade of grass with perfection.

You should be able to turn on and off the switch of perfectionism. Sometimes it's needed, and sometimes it's not. Don't make a default setting of always being a perfectionist. Change it according to circumstances. Don't hide your laziness with perfection.

Here is an excellent quote by Shane Parish:

"If a decision is reversible, make it as soon as possible. If it is irreversible, make it as late as possible".

Done is better than perfect

Not all things can be done perfectly. You can't sit there and spend days on a task that can be done in a few minutes. Lazy people always do this when they finally decide to start working on a project, and they start worrying about all the tiny details. They get so overwhelmed by the details that they never even begin doing it.

Don't be Mediocre!

"Mediocrity doesn't just happen. It's chosen over time through small choices day by day."

–Todd Henry

We always have the choice of becoming great or becoming mediocre. To become great, it's not an easy task. You have to give your very best each day. There will be failures. You will struggle a lot. To become mediocre, you don't have to do anything; your goal in life is never to be an average person. You must give your best. Mediocre people never give their best they settle down once things are a little bit okay, or they know that if they keep going things will become hard.

99% of the people settle for less than they want. They settle for the jobs they hate, and then they wonder why they aren't productive, are not happy, lack motivation, and don't wake up with the energy to do their job.

How can you wake up happy doing something you hate?

"Your work will fill a large part of your life, and the only way to be truly satisfied is to do what you believe is great work. And the only way to do great work is to love what you do. If you haven't found it yet, keep looking. Don't settle. As with all matters of the heart, you'll know when you find it."

-Steve Jobs

Nobody wants to be mediocre. If you don't believe it, ask someone, "Do you want to become mediocre?". You will get the answer. The answer is always going to be no.

The one big reason people are mediocre is everyone around them is also mediocre. And if you try to become a little bit ambitious, people will tell you all sorts of things to destroy your ambition. They don't want to shine. Maybe they want you to, but if you aren't mediocre, it will make them feel bad inside their heart, knowing they're wasting their human potential.

When we are children, we have all sorts of dreams and aspirations, and then something happens, and everybody falls in love with mediocrity.

People have no sense of energy inside them to do something that time is passing by and they're just dragging through life instead of living it.

Think big.

Even if you fail, that will still be better than the regret of never trying to push your boundaries. Imagine being an 80-year-old wishing you could travel the world, pursue your dreams, and live how you want to, not how other people want to.

You still have time. At least for now, you have it, but one day, there will be no time to do anything. Death will be standing at your door.

Live your life always doing what you want to. You will need no productivity tips; you will stop being lazy because a sense of purpose will be inside you.

If you don't like your work, change your work.

Library Mindset

If you don't like your friends, change your friends.

If you don't like your thinking, change your thinking.

If you don't like your life, change your life.

Remember that a life of greatness is harder than life of mediocracy. It's not easy, but the path will be worth it.

The Myth of Multitasking

"The man who chases two rabbits catches neither."

- Confucius

On December 11, 1998, NASA launched the Mars Climate Orbiter to study the climate of Mars. The Mars Climate Orbiter cost $125 million to build. On September 23, 1999, the spacecraft entered orbit with Mars, and then suddenly, NASA lost contact with it. It was due to a simple error: engineers failed to convert from English units to metric. The spacecraft got too close to Mars, and it was destroyed.

Multitasking means doing more than one thing at a time. It sounds good, but it doesn't work. We can't focus on multiple important things at the same time. If you have two important tasks, then multitasking will reduce your efficiency. You're also more likely to tire quickly if you switch tasks continuously.

As the saying goes "The devil is in the details "You need to have complete focus on whatever you're doing at the moment. Switching tasks will reduce your focus, and you're more likely to make tiny mistakes that can have a huge impact.

The more you switch from one task to another, the faster you will get tired; when you're tired, you're less likely to pay attention to tiny details. The level of stress also rises as we change tasks.

3 Tips That Will Make You More Productive:

1)Avoid switching tasks. Work on one task with complete focus and then move to another task.

2)Remove all distractions you can from the work you're doing. Be completely focused on the task at hand.

3)Turn off all the non-important notifications on your phone.

Focus

The best thing you can do to improve your productivity is to focus on one task at a time. Important things aren't meant to be done with low focus. They demand our complete focus. Let's say you need to do three things. The best way is to do one with complete focus and then move to the second and third. The worst way is trying to do all the things at one time and switching your task every five minutes to do another task. You might feel that you're productive, but you are not. Don't allow anything to interrupt your focus.

Take a Nap

When you work for an extended period with focus, your mind energy will get reduced. The best thing you can do is to take a nap. It may not be possible for everybody, but if you can do it, then it's worth it; you will be more energized to work with more focus. Don't go for a long nap instead opt for shorter ones less than an hour. Avoid taking a nap after 3 pm. You may find it difficult to sleep. Also, if you sleep too much during the day, you may have trouble sleeping at night.

No Interruptions

We work best when we aren't constantly disturbed by others. It takes some time for our mind to get into a flow state to achieve maximum output, and if you're constantly distracted by things, you will not be able to focus properly, and your productivity will suffer.

Most Important Thing

If you must do multiple things first, you must know which one is important. You must remove all the non-important tasks that will not help you achieve your goals.

In everyone's life, there are a couple of things that you can stop doing, and it wouldn't make any difference. The biggest distraction people face is that instead of doing the important thing, they start doing the nonimportant thing.

Daily Routine

"You'll never change your life until you change something you do daily. The secret of your success is found in your daily routine." - John C. Maxwell

Developing a daily routine is super important. You must have some routine that you would follow. Without a proper routine, you won't be consistent with your work. Some days, you would be motivated and work well; the rest of the days, you would lack motivation, and you're going to procrastinate.

A daily routine would help you stay consistent. It will make you more focused and will help you finish important tasks. Without routine, we prefer doing the easy task, not the important one.

What you do daily is going to shape your future. You are the sum of everything you've done for the past few years. To change who you are, you must change what you do daily.

A routine helps your mind to stop thinking all the time about what to do next. You can adjust your routine to make it as perfect as possible. I suggest you do it right now: look back at yesterday and see what can be improved.

Here is the daily routine of Leo Tolstoy:

Leo Tolstoy was born on 9 September 1828. When he was 18, he started "Journal of Daily Activities". In this journal, he would write how much time he would spend on any task like writing or studying, and then he would later comment on how well he performed.

He would wake up each day at five o'clock. He would take a walk for an hour. He has a strict habit of writing each day. He also slept around 2 hours during the day. He used to work in complete isolation. And would go to bed no later than 10 o'clock.

When should you wake up?

There is a ton of advice on when one should wake up. From 4 am to 9 am, everyone has a different opinion. You must listen to yourself and don't lie to yourself because you can make all sorts of excuses to justify your decision.

Think for a moment and ask yourself what is the best time for me to wake up, which will make me more productive and help me achieve my goals. Don't say you must wake up late because you want to be comfortable. You need to choose on behalf of your future self.

Make the right choice, not the easy one.

Sit Alone

"All of humanity's problems stem from our inability to sit quietly in a room alone" - Blaise Pascal

You must sit alone and think about what you are doing with your life, what things you're doing are not improving your life, and instead, making your life worse. Do this simple daily exercise for 5-10 minutes, and you will have fantastic clarity about your life.

Eliminate All Distractions

The Trojan was between the Greeks and the City of Troy. It was a great battle. It continued for ten years. But in the end, the Greeks won the war with the famous Trojan Horse. They built a giant wooden horse that was hollow from the inside and left it outside the gates of Troy, and the whole army of Greeks left. Trojans thought that they left the war and accepted defeat. They pulled the horse inside the Walls of Troy. When the night fell, the best warriors of the Greeks, who were hidden inside the Trojan Horse, got out and opened the gates for their army, which now sailed back. Troy has fallen.

Distractions are like the Trojan Horse. They destroy your focus and productivity. Be completely aware of hidden distractions. Distractions are costly. Even if something distracted you for 2 minutes, 10 minutes are wasted because refocusing takes time.

Delete Apps

On everyone's phones, a few apps distract them, are addicting, and you constantly waste time on them.

The Art of Laziness

Delete them. Delete them all. If any app distracts you, it should be deleted. For most, it would be video games. Once they open the game, they waste 15 minutes before realizing it. Relaxation is not bad. Everyone should relax as much as they like, but video games aren't built for relaxation. They consume much mental energy, so you're even more tired after playing. There are better ways to relax.

Do this right now: open your phone and review all the apps and games you waste your time on. Delete them. If you need them later, you can always download them again. This simple thing will at least save you from wasting 30 minutes every day.

Learn To Say No

"Half of the troubles of this life can be traced to saying yes too quickly and not saying no soon enough."

-Josh Billings

If you want to take better control of your life and time, then you must learn how to say no when you want to say no. We often say yes, even if we don't want to, just because we don't want to make the other person sad. You accept everything other people want you to do, but you only have finite energy and time. If you say yes to every opportunity, invite, and work you're asked to do, you will soon start to feel burdened by it. To appease others, you will lose yourself in the process.

Say no when you want to.

Say yes when you want to.

This is the only way to take back charge of your time.

You don't have to be rude to say no. You can say it very politely when you want to. I also don't say that you have to say no to everything. That's also bad. You need to know when to say yes and when to say no.

Your time is valuable and if you keep doing what others want you to do then you will be distracted from your main goal and, instead, start doing side things which will lower your productivity. If we keep listening to others, then we will have no time to listen to ourselves.

We need to learn how to say no to opportunities that we have no interest in, and if we try to do everything, we will get nothing done. As the saying goes, to be everywhere is to be nowhere.

If you're saying yes to everything, then there is a chance that you're not focused on your goals, or you have no goals, which is even worse. If you have no goals, you will get pushed by others according to their will here and there.

Here is an excellent quote by Seneca:

"If you don't know what port you sail to, no wind is favorable."

Don't Work 24/7

"20 years from now, the only people who will remember you worked late are your kids."

- Sahil Bloom

The goal of becoming more productive is not to work more, but it's the opposite. The goal is to get your work done in less time so that you can spend time with your friends and family. If you work too long, then both your creativity and productivity suffer. It's not worth it to spend 12 hours every day in the office and neglect all other aspects of your life. Sometimes, it's okay, but not all the time.

We should measure productivity by how much work we get done, not by how much time we spend.

Some people spend more time in the office to satisfy their ego.

If you're working a lot and still aren't achieving your goals, there is a high chance that you're avoiding the important things that need to be done instead of doing things that aren't that important. The less important things are distracting you from doing the actual important things. Doing less essential things instead of the most important thing is also procrastination. Don't procrastinate on the essential things. They will bring most of the results you want to achieve.

I have seen that people do this deliberately; the essential things are hard to do, so instead of doing the hard work, they start doing easy things that make them appear busy.

Life is Short

Life is very short. Don't waste all your life working and then when you're old wishing you did things differently.

Think about all the things you will regret when you're old. Enjoy your life. You may never get a chance to do the things you can do now. You can't enjoy travel when you're 80.

Less is More

If you work a lot and still are not able to achieve your goals, there could be two reasons:

1. You may not be working as hard as you think. You may be lazy most of the time and think you're working hard.

2. You may be working on the wrong things. You could be working on less important things. Things that don't matter that much. You spend most of your time on minor things but don't do the challenging and essential things.

Everything you do has some value that you will gain from doing it. Some tasks have more value in your life than others. You don't want to get distracted by less important tasks. You want to dedicate as much time as possible to the things that matter.

Be Productive, Not Busy

"If the ladder is not leaning against the right wall, every step we take just gets us to the wrong place faster." - Stephen Covey

Working for 12 hours doesn't mean anything if you are working on the wrong things. You should work on things that move you toward your goals. Don't start climbing a ladder and then halfway you look around and realise that you're climbing the wrong ladder. Work on your own dreams, not the dreams of others.

Be productive, not busy. There is no reward for being busy all the time. Don't be busy just for the sake of being busy. Be productive instead. Work on things that move you towards your goals, not away.

Don't Wait

"Wisdom is knowing what to do next; Skill is knowing how to do it, and Virtue is doing it." - David Starr Jordan

The one main reason that a lot of people are lazy is they're always waiting for the right time so that they can do something, and guess what? The right time never happens. No time is good or bad. You can start today and make some progress, or you can wait and console yourself that your time will come.

Throw away all the garbage that eventually your time will come without putting in the work. It won't happen; you must do the work to achieve your goals. I have seen zero successful people who just waited for the perfect time.

Yes, some tasks can't be done faster no matter how hard you try but that doesn't mean that you shouldn't try at all and keep waiting.

Don't confuse your laziness with patience. Patience and laziness are very different. Don't mix them. You must put in the work every day, and then you should be patient with the results.

A Story of Great Patience

A farmer once planted a bamboo tree. The farmer watered the crop daily for a year but saw no sign of life. No growth, no sprouts, no hope. The second year was the same as the third and fourth years. His patience and faith in this "miracle" bamboo plant faded. During the fifth year, just as he was about to give up on his dream of growing the plant, he noticed it sprout. The bamboo sprung up 60 feet over the next six weeks!

This is an excellent story of both patience and hard work. Life is just like this. There is no overnight success. It takes a long time for success to happen, but this also doesn't mean sitting there and doing nothing. The crop didn't grow independently; the farmer had to plant it, take care of it, and be patient.

Impatient With Action and Patient with Results

A student of Zen went to his teacher and asked earnestly, "I am devoted to studying Zen. How long will it take me to master it?"

"Ten years," the teacher said.

Impatiently, the student answered, "But I want to master it faster than that. I will work very hard. I will practice every day for ten or more hours if necessary. How long will it take then?"

The teacher thought for a moment, "20 years."

You have no control over the results you get or not get. You can only control your actions and the work you do. Everyone wants to get results fast when they're working hard, thinking they should be rewarded right now for their work, but generally, that doesn't happen. You may work hard for years before you get the results you want. You must be patient with the results, but don't be patient with action.

Don't be one of those people who think everything will be given to them automatically. You must do the work first before you get the results you want.

"A man who is a master of patience is master of everything else." - George Savile

No Perfect Time

There is nothing as perfect timing to start anything new. You can start today and make some progress, or you can keep waiting for the ideal time. The perfect time is now. There is no better time than today to start moving toward your goals. Stop being lazy and start doing the work that is required.

Consistency Is Key

To be great at anything, you must do it daily and for a long time.

To become a better painter, you need to paint every day.

To become a better writer, you need to write every day.

To become a better speaker, you need to speak every day.

Most people never start; some start but give up as soon as things get complicated; only a few are consistent and show up every day, no matter how hard it gets.

It Will Get Easy

"It may seem difficult at first, but everything is difficult at first." - Miyamoto Musashi

The hardest thing is to start. That's where 95% of people are stuck. They never start. They keep waiting and making excuses. If you want to break a bad habit the first few days will be the hardest and after a few weeks, it will get pretty easy to keep going.

Do What You Say

If you love to procrastinate, you will not honor your words. If you say that you're going to something and then you don't do it, then soon people will stop trusting you. I don't mean to do everything that other people ask you to do, but when you finally say that you're going to do something, then you better do it. If you say from tomorrow, you're going to the gym, then no matter what happens, you better go to the gym. Do what you say. Stop saying things and then just be lazy. Honor your word and do the things you say.

Surround Yourself with the Right People

"You are the average of the five persons you spend the most time with." - Jim Rohn

If your friends are lazy, then you'll be lazy

If your friends procrastinate, you'll also procrastinate.

If you're friends work hard, you'll also work hard.

If your friends read books, you'll also start reading books.

There may be an outlier, but that's very rare. The main reason people are lazy is because whoever they spend most of their time is also lazy. You adopt the habits of the person who is very close to you. Their good or bad habits become yours. If your friend likes to waste time, you'll also join him in wasting time. It's tough not to get influenced by other people.

So, what you can do? The only thing you can do is to be aware of what you're doing. Only by awareness can you conquer your laziness and procrastination. You must be very aware of your actions. You must learn to say no.

This thing also goes the other way if you have friends who are not lazy, don't procrastinate, and have adopted good habits. You'll become like them.

The choice is yours. The people you surround yourself will have a massive impact on your life. They will shape your thoughts, actions, and your life. The right people will improve your life, and the wrong ones will worsen your life.

If you're always with a negative person, they will make you a negative person but instead of you surround yourself with positive people you will become a positive person. You must think about whom you're surrounding yourself with.

Change Your Circle to Change Your Thinking

If you want to change your thoughts, you must change everything you do. You must change the people you hang around with. If the people you spend the most time with are lazy, negative, and in no way make your life even slightly better, then it would be worth it to change your circle or reduce listening to their advice.

Someone said,

"Close the window that hurt you, no matter how beautiful the view is," and I felt that!

Don't Take Advice from Everyone

Don't take advice on matters from someone you dislike exchanging places with. Let's say you want advice on how to be happier; the last person you want to take this advice from is an unhappy person. Think about it: if his advice has some value, then why would he be unhappy? Nobody loves to remain unhappy.

Library Mindset

Who you take advice from will decide the life you're going to live.

- Take advice from unhappy people, and you will become unhappy.
- Take advice from unhealthy people, and you will become an unhealthy person.
- Take advice from angry people, and you will become angry.

"If they don't have what you want, don't listen to what they say." – Alex Hormozi

Stop taking advice from people you don't want to become. Stop listening to other people's opinions about how you should live your life and what you should do. Their advice is completely useless.

It's your life; live the way you want to.

Don't Worry

"I am an old man and have known many troubles, most of which never happened."

-Mark Twain

Worrying loves a lazy person because a lazy person has nothing else to do except worry. Since they aren't doing any work, all they can do is worry about the future. If you believe in yourself, then there is no need to worry. When you don't believe in yourself? The worry starts to appear. All types of negative thoughts start to enter your mind. You start worrying about things with a very low chance of happening.

Worrying can only be destroyed by one thing, and that is through action.

That's the only way I know to make your worries go away. I have no other knowledge. Let's say you're worried about your health, and then the only thing

Library Mindset

you can do is to start taking care of your health. There is nothing else you can do. Thinking about your health all day will not make you healthier; it might do the opposite.

Worrying is natural. We all worry about jobs, business, health, money, family, etc. You must classify your worries into two parts:

1) The things that you can control, and you can do something about it.

2) The things you can't control, and you can't do anything about them.

Worrying about the first part is okay. You have to worry about your health so that you can take some action and improve it. This is what I call good worrying. It helps you do things that can make your life better.

Worrying about the second part is stupid. Why worry about something you can't control? Let's say tomorrow, an asteroid is coming to Earth and going to kill all of us. What's the worry? You can't do anything. Worrying about things you can't control is going to rob your happiness.

The Art of Laziness

Make a new rule to never worry about anything that you can't control, and if you can control it, then act immediately and do something about it. In both cases, there should be no worry.

Do the Hard Thing First

"The cold water doesn't get warmer if you jump late."

-Unknown

Here's a simple tip to become more productive and feel better: the hardest work you have for the entire day should be done first. No matter how hard it is, it needs to be done first. Whenever you start working, write all the things that need to be done, pick the hardest and most complicated task, and immediately start doing the task.

As humans, we don't like to be uncomfortable; we don't like to do hard things if possible. So, we avoid it, but you can't avoid doing a task. If you can avoid doing a task, it wasn't important in the first place. But if a task is important and needs to be done, the best thing you can do is to start working on the task as soon as possible.

The hard task is also important and will help you achieve your goals. But since it's hard, you wouldn't like to do it first, and then procrastination will take over you, and you would delay it by saying, "I'm too tired" or "I don't have time now." These are just excuses to avoid doing the work that needs to be done.

Hard Choices = Easy Life

Everyone wants to live an easy life with no worries. A life where you don't have to do anything that you don't want to do. A life in which there is complete freedom to do anything you want to. A life in which you don't have to worry about anything. Who doesn't want to live like this?

An easy life for most people can only be possible by making hard choices. There is no other way. You have the option to choose one of the following:

Easy Choices = Hard Life

Hard Choices = Easy Life

This is the harsh truth of life. You have to make hard choices in the short term to live an easy life in the long term. Being lazy is easy in the short run, but it will make your life harder in the long run. Doing is hard; not doing is even harder. Going to the gym is hard, but not being healthy is even harder.

The choice is yours; you can make hard choices to live an easy life or easy choices to live a hard life.

Do What You Need To

There is a very fine line between doing what you love and doing what you find easy to do. We, as humans, love to do what is easy. We run away from doing hard things. But once you start doing hard things, then it will get easier. The start is always the hardest. There is no reward in life for doing the easy thing. In life, you will be rewarded for how hard things you can do. Everybody can do the easy thing. It's the hard things that count. To get better results, start doing hard things.

Stop Living a Balance Life

I'm not telling you to become crazy, but there is so much laziness in our life that as soon as things get a little bit hard, we stop doing them by saying we want to live a balanced life. You can balance a lot more than you think.

Balance is required in life. You need to sleep a good amount of time according to your body's needs. You need to spend as much time as you like with your family and friends.

To live a balanced life, we have to remove all the hard things from life. We don't even like to do anything hard. We don't want to make hard choices. We don't want to try new things. We just want to let things happen as they're happening.

A little bit of unbalance is required to achieve great things. I'm not in favor of sacrificing anything for anything. I don't suggest you sacrifice your health for money or anything else. All I'm saying is that you try to push a little bit of those imaginary walls that you have created in your mind. Pushing them will not cost you anything. If you don't feel good, you can always move back but don't sit there and never even try to push the wall a little bit.

Picture Your Future Self

Whenever you're feeling lazy and don't want to do the work, start thinking about your future self.

How will you feel about not doing it in the future? How will you handle the regret?

Now imagine how your life will look in the future if you do the hard work instead of procrastinating.

There is no better way to motivate yourself than to think about your future self. Your future is always created by you in the present. The actions you take will reflect how your future will look.

"People do not decide their futures; they decide their habits, and their habits decide their futures."

— *F. M. Alexander*

Delegate

If you want to do a few small things right, do them yourself. Learn to delegate if you want to do great things and make a big impact. - John C. Maxwell

There is no way to do everything by yourself. No matter what technique, hack, or tips you try, there will never be enough time to do everything by yourself, and that's a good thing because we don't need to do everything by ourselves. Other people can help us do the things we don't have time to do.

If you have any task that needs to be done and you have no time to do it, it's a low-value task, which means that even if you don't do it by yourself and instead hire someone else, it will not make a difference.

Many things take a lot of your time that aren't that important, but you can delegate right now so that you can use the time to do the things you want to do.

Make a list of all the non-important tasks you need to do every day, how much time it takes to do them, and how much money it will take for someone else to do them. You will see that you're doing things that can be easily outsourced and very cheaply that take a lot of time daily. Try this for a few things, and then see how it goes. Even if somebody else does around 90% of a good job, it's worth it. Also, there is a high chance that somebody else will do a better job than us. We think that we can do a better job, but that's not true. It may appear to our mind that we can do better, but most of the time, that's not the case.

How To Learn Anything Faster

"I constantly see people rise in life who are not the smartest, sometimes not even the most diligent, but they are learning machines." - Charlie Munger

Learn What Is Useful

Don't learn anything just for the sake of learning it. Learn things that can improve your life. Don't become so weird with learning things that you start learning local languages spoken in some villages in the nowhere. Think about what you're learning, whether that is useful or not. If not, don't spend time learning it. There are thousands of things that you can learn today that are helpful and will improve your life.

No Laziness While Learning

You can't be lazy if you're trying to learn something. You can't just sit there and keep waiting to learn. You need to learn now. You need to start right now. Let's say you want to learn how to code. You can start learning right now. There is no need to wait. Speed is crucial. I'm not saying to watch videos at 3x, but you must have a sense of urgency. Learn at whatever pace you're comfortable with, but start it now. You will thank yourself later.

Speed Reading

"If you can speed read it, it isn't worth reading." – Naval Ravikant

The Art of Laziness

I'm not a huge fan of speed-reading books, as great books worth reading demand your complete attention. The fastest way to read more books is to spend more time on books. That's it. There are some books I spent weeks and some that I even read in a day. Don't think too much about reading speeds. If you're a beginner, it will get better over time. Focus more on the quality of the books you read. Also, stop reading the same type of books. Read a variety of books. Don't stick to the same type of books.

Read fiction.

Read non-fiction

Read self-help.

Read history.

Read philosophy.

Read biographies.

Read Autobiographies.

Read everything.

Part 2
Tips & Techniques

"The tragedy in life doesn't lie in not reaching your goal. The tragedy lies in having no goal to reach."

– Benjamin E. Mays

20 Productivity Tips I Wish I Had Known Earlier

1. Plan your day. Write everything you want to achieve in a day.

2. Write your goals on a physical paper.

3. Follow the 80/20 Rule. 20% of your work will bring you 80% of your results.

4. Stop Multitasking. Switching tasks reduce your productivity a lot.

5. Focus on one task at a time.

6. Remove all the distractions from your environment.

7. When tired, take a nap.

9. Learn to say no. You will never have enough time if you say yes to everything.

Library Mindset

10. Delegate all the non-important tasks.

11. Don't wait for the perfect time. Do It Now.

12. Anything that can be done in under 5 minutes should be done now.

13. Do the task that you hate first.

14. Set deadlines; the task will never be finished without deadlines.

15. Stop focusing on things that don't help you achieve your goals.

16. Don't become a perfectionist when it's not required.

17. Schedule a time when you're going to check your email.

18. Avoid all the unnecessary meetings.

19. Avoid negative people at all costs.

20. Do what you love.

80/20 Rule

This is also called the Pareto Principle. This means 20% of your work will bring you 80% of the results.

There are many things you can do each day, but there are a few things that are important and will bring the most results, and there are other things that are less important and will not help us achieve our goals.

Even if you don't procrastinate, you should still be very aware of what you're doing because if you're doing things that are not valuable and will not help you achieve your goals, you're wasting your time.

Think for a moment. What is the most important thing you can do to help you achieve your goals?

It's probably hard to do, but it would be worth doing. The goal is not to be busy always but to do what needs to be done.

The Parkinson's Law

This was introduced by Cyril Northcote Parkinson. The law means that the work expands to fill the time allotted for completion. So, if you allow yourself 2 hours to finish a task, it will take 2 hours, but if you only have 1 hour, you will find a way to complete the task in an hour. This is great if you cannot start a project or it takes too long to complete.

8 Japanese Techniques to Overcome Laziness

1. IKIGAI

It means to have a purpose in life. The reason you wake up each working excited to do something. When you have a purpose, you won't feel lazy or unmotivated.

4 Rules of IKIGAI:

1) Do what you love,

2) Do what you're good at,

3) Do what the world needs,

4) Do what you can be paid for.

2. Kaizen

It means focusing on small improvements every day and not waiting for big improvements but trying to become 1% better every day. Instead of setting a big goal, we should divide it into multiple small goals and tackle each of them one by one.

3. Shoshin

It's a concept from Zen Buddhism that means approaching things with a beginner's mindset.

"If your mind is empty ... It is open to everything. In the beginner's mind, there are many possibilities, but in the expert's mind, there are few." - Shunryu Suzuki (author of Zen Mind, Beginner's Mind)

4. Hara Hachi Bu

This means to stop eating after you're 80% full. If you eat too much, you're more likely to feel lazy. This happens to people all the time. Once they eat their lunch, they start to feel tired because the body tries to digest all the food they eat. So you start to feel sleepy, and you will not love to work instead you would like to procrastinate.

5. Shinrin-yoku

Shinin in Japanese means "forest," and yoku means "bath."

It means that one should spend more time with nature. Spending time with nature is the best way to deal with stress. Whenever you're feeling stressed or overwhelmed, go for a walk.

6. Wabi-sabi

This means that instead of perfection, one should find beauty in imperfection. Things can't be perfect all the time. Some things can't be perfect, and that's okay. There is beauty even in perfection. Love the things the way they are. Don't be stubborn and try to change them. You will ruin their beauty.

7. Ganbaru

Nothing worth doing takes much time, no matter how hard one tries.

One should be patient with the results and still try to do the best that can be done.

8. Gaman

It means to show patience and perseverance when things go hard. When you go on a journey it's not going to be all pleasant there will be a lot of times when things will go wrong. You will face many difficulties when you start doing the things you want to do. There will be failures.

Do This For 10 Minute Before You Sleep

Every day is important. You need to both move forward and look back. You must reflect on your actions to check whether you're doing the right things. And if you're doing the right things, how can they be improved?

You can never improve something that you can't track. There are a lot of small distractions throughout the day that can lower your productivity and don't even make your life better. So, here's what you must do every night before you go to sleep:

Library Mindset

1)Take a pen and paper and write whatever you have accomplished throughout the day. Write down all the good and bad things you did throughout the day. Do it hour by hour, and you will see how much time you wasted on things that didn't improve your life even a tiny bit.

2)Write down the things that you're going to do tomorrow. Make a short to-do list. Don't make it too long. Planning your day is super important. It keeps you focused on the important tasks so you don't get distracted by less important tasks.

This simple exercise every day will make you aware of how you're spending your time every day, where you're wasting your time, and how you can remove those distractions from your life that don't add any value.

3 Arrows

You will feel exhausted if you try to do too many things in a day. There is nothing wrong with being exhausted but the problem is that when you try to do too many things generally you start doing the things that aren't that valuable. You start doing tasks that will not move you toward your goals.

So, what you need to do is to write the things you have to do. Then you must cut all the non-important things. You can only do three high-value tasks. What are those three things going to be?

10 Tiny Habits That Will Change Your Life

1. Move Your Body

Our bodies are not made to sit all day. If you don't do any physical work, then you will feel tired all the time. Move your body every day, no matter whether it's physical work or some sort of exercise. Go for a run early in the morning or when you feel overwhelmed during work go for a walk.

2. You Are What You Eat

What you eat will impact the way you feel during the day. If you feel lethargic, then maybe you need to change what you eat. It depends on person to person, so look at your diet and see whether you can improve it.

3. Have A Purpose

If you have no purpose, then you will never have the energy to do anything. If you don't love your work, then you will not be excited or filled with energy. You need to have a sense of purpose to have constant motivation to work hard. Find a purpose in your life.

4. Drink More Water

Make sure that you're drinking plenty of water throughout the day.

5. Surround Yourself with People You Love

Be around with people you love and care about. People around whom you feel happy and blissful. Stop being around negative people. Move away from all the toxic people in your life.

6. Take Risks

If you're not taking risks, then you will not have the motivation to do things. Our mind needs constant challenges to keep it alert, and if you're doing the same task over and over, then your motivation will decrease.

7. Don't Overload Yourself

Stop having unrealistic expectations of yourself. You need to push yourself but if you do it too much then it will have negative effects. Stop trying to do too many things in a day. You can't do 20 things in a day.

8. Not Multitasking

Multitasking is a lie. It exhausts you fast and doesn't allow you to focus on a task. It acts as a distraction. Switching tasks reduce your productivity instead of boosting it. Don't multitask.

9. Eliminating All Distractions

The best thing you can do is to eliminate all the distractions from your environment. Anything that diverts your brain's energy should be eliminated.

10. Having a Sense of Urgency

You can't achieve anything in your life if you don't have a sense of urgency. You need to be patient with results and inpatient with action. Anything that you need to do should be done as fast as possible.

Pomodoro Technique

This technique is very simple what you need to do is: work for 25 minutes uninterrupted then take a break for 5 minutes and you will repeat that.

I like to go for a long time before taking a break. You must see this for yourself when you're getting tired, and you should adjust this technique accordingly. Rest is very important, during your work you should take rest whenever you feel you're tired mentally due to working for a long period or working intensively.

If you're fully into any task, then you may have noticed that you stop worrying about everything else; you stop noticing the passage of time. This may not happen often, but when it happens, you feel happy. This joy can happen only if you're doing something that you like. You can't feel this if you don't like your work. Loving your work is the only way to feel this.

5 Minute Rule

You always have a lot of pending tasks because you tend to procrastinate even on small tasks that can be done instantly or in under 5 minutes, and you say that you will do it later. And you never do it and the list of things to do keeps getting larger and larger and then you feel overwhelmed by the substantial number of pending tasks that need to be done.

And then you get nothing done because doing one or two things will not do much.

A new rule you should always follow is that whatever can be done under 5 minutes should be done now. You cannot delay the task for tomorrow. It must be done now.

As Benjamin Franklin said, *"Beware of little expenses - a small leak will sink a great ship."*

In the same way, we should be very aware of little things to do because they will destroy our productivity.

Do this one thing right now: list all the small things you need to do. Close this book and do everything that can be done right now.

Do it. Don't wait. Waiting means the work can't be done automatically. You must do the work whether you do it now or later.

Two Day Rule

The two-day rule is simple: you would not miss anything for two days straight. You can miss it for one day if you must but never for two days. Let's say you started exercising every day, then suddenly, you have an emergency and can't train for a day. That is completely okay but if you miss two days in a row then not exercising becomes your habit and there is a chance that you may not exercise for many days.

Consistency is very important. Without consistency, you can't move toward your goals. If you have a car it needs to be looked after otherwise issues will start rising, it may not start when you need it or may stop in the middle of your journey.

Wake Up!

"When you arise in the morning, think of what a precious privilege it is to be alive, to breathe, to think, to enjoy, to love." - Marcus Aurelius

The time for you to do the things that you want to do is running out. You must always live with a sense of urgency. We have a very short time left. I don't want to make you feel sad or anxious.

Wake up; you will get the same results if you keep doing your current work. You must change what you do to change the results you want.

The life you want to live is on the other side of laziness. Living each day with complete awareness, enjoying each moment, and not living in the future or past but in the present. Your future can only be changed by the things you do in the present.

Library Mindset

Each day is important.

Each hour is important.

Each moment is important.

Don't live your life by the expectations of other people. You will always regret that in the future. Why did you listen to other people and not listen to your inner voice, who was trying to guide you to the right path?

If you're a 30-year-old and you're going to live up to the age of 90, you have already spent $1/3^{rd}$ of your life. If you're happy by the way, you spent your previous day then great but if you don't like your past then you must do the things that need to be done so when you're 70 you don't say that I have wasted my entire life.

Drop everything holding you back from living your life the way you want. Don't worry about other people's opinions. They didn't live happily and want you to do the same. They're filled with regrets and want you to have the same kind of regrets.

Once, a father and a son were coming back from a village far away, where they had purchased a donkey. They overheard a man saying, see the fools, they have a donkey but still walking on feet. Both thought it was a good idea, and they sat on the donkey.

The Art of Laziness

On their way, another villager saw and spoke. Look, look at the poor donkey. He can hardly walk. The man felt sorry for the donkey and got off. While crossing the fields, a woman remarked. The son is young and healthy; he should walk and let his father sit on the donkey. Son told his father, "I am sorry, Dad, please come sit on the donkey," so they changed places.

As they were about to reach their village, a passerby said, "Hey, see the selfish man; the poor son is walking and enjoying the ride. Without giving another thought, both tied the donkey upside down to a long bamboo and carried him through the village.

By the time they reached home, all were laughing at them. A villager elder asked, why are you carrying this donkey like this? Can't walk?

Father explained what happened on the way. The old man said everyone was laughing at you because instead of using your senses, you kept on doing what others said.

One day just like this book your life will end. Do the things you want to do. Travel the places you want to. Read the books you want to. Surround yourself with the people you want to.

Time is running out. Start living!

Notes

- Andrei, V. (n.d.). Retrieved from The Sovereign Artist: https://vizi.substack.com/

- Aureilius, M. (n.d.). *Meditations.* Modern Library.

- Bezos, J. (n.d.). *2016 Letter to Shareholders.* Retrieved from Amazon: https://www.aboutamazon.com/news/company-news/2016-letter-to-shareholders

- Billings, J. (2023). *The Complete Works of Josh Billings.* Good Press.

- Bloom, S. (2023, March 3). Retrieved from X: https://twitter.com/SahilBloom/status/1631281464313610246?

- Bloom, S. (2023, May 17). Retrieved from X:

https://twitter.com/SahilBloom/status/1658809456375857153?

- Churchill, W. (1943, September 6). *Winston Churchill's Honorary Degree Speech.* Retrieved from Harvard Magazine: https://www.harvardmagazine.com/2018/09/churchill-harvard-september-6-1943

- Epictetus. (2008). *Discourses and Selected Writings.* Penguin Publishing Group.

- Franklin, B. (1757). *The Way to Wealth.*

- Fuggle, L. (2023, September 23). *Tolstoy's 'Rules of Life,' Perfectionism and Constant Self-Improvement.* Retrieved from Tolstoy Therapy: https://tolstoytherapy.com/tolstoys-rules-and-perfectionism/

- Hormozi, A. (2023, June 19). Retrieved from X: https://twitter.com/AlexHormozi/status/1670518034006507522

- Isaacson, W. (2011). *Steve Jobs.* Thorndike Press.

- Isaacson, W. (2017). *Leonardo Da Vinci.* Simon and Schuster.

- Jobs, S. (2005, June 12). *Steve Jobs' 2005 Stanford Commencement Address.* Retrieved from YouTube: https://www.youtube.com/watch?v=UF8uR6Z6KLc

- Koch, R. (1999). *The 80/20 Principle, Expanded and Updated: The Secret to Achieving More with Less.* Crown.

- Life, T. A. (2011). *Tolstoy: A Russian Life.* Houghton Mifflin Harcourt.

- Musashi, M. (n.d.). *The Book of Five Rings.*

- Orbiter, M. C. (1999). *Mars Climate Orbiter.* Retrieved from NASA: https://science.nasa.gov/mission/mars-climate-orbiter/

- Parrish, S. (2020, June 29). Retrieved from X: https://twitter.com/shaneaparrish/status/1277415631965519873

- Progress, P. L. (1986). *Parkinson's Law.* Penguin.

- Rohn, J. (n.d.).

- Seneca. (2004). *Letters from a Stoic.* Penguin Books.

- Steven Naifeh, G. W. (2012). *Van Gogh: The Life.* Random House Publishing Group.

- Zuckerberg, M. (2011). Interview with Mark Zuckerberg at Startup School in 2011.

Made in United States
North Haven, CT
08 January 2024